# Why are teddy bears called Teddy?

Disney BOOKS BY MAIL

**DK Direct Limited**
**Managing Art Editor** Eljay Crompton
**Senior Editor** Rosemary McCormick
**Writer** Alexandra Parsons
**Illustrators** The Alvin White Studios and Richard Manning
**Designers** Wayne Blades, Veneta Bullen, Richard Clemson,
Sarah Goodwin, Diane Klein, Sonia Whillock

# Contents

# Why are yo-yos called yo-yos?

The word yo-yo means "come-back" in a language spoken in the Philippines. Five hundred years ago, in the Philippines, the yo-yo was used as a toy AND as a fighting weapon. A toy very like the yo-yo was also used in Greece 3,000 years ago. So people have been yo-yoing for a long time!

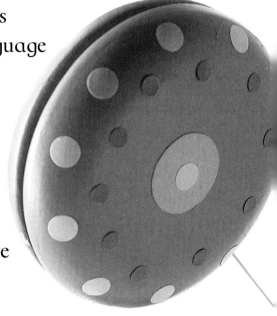

**Yo-yo masters**
People everywhere enjoy playing with yo-yos. There are even competitions to see who can yo-yo the best.

## Yo-yo facts

☞ The yo-yo we use now is based on the modern yo-yo designed in the United States in the 1920s by Donald F. Duncan. Thank you, Donald.

☞ The original Filipino fighting yo-yo weighed four pounds and the string was 20 feet long. Try looping the loop with that!

**Tricky tricks**
There are lots of tricks you can do with a yo-yo. You can "loop the loop," "walk the dog," or do a "whirlwind"!

**Up, down**
Did you hear about the ship carrying a cargo of yo-yos?
**It sank 53 times.**

# Who invented roller skates?

A Belgian musician named Joseph Merlin, in 1760. He wanted to impress guests at a dinner party, so he decided to make his entry on wheels – playing a violin! Unfortunately, once Mr. Merlin got rolling, he couldn't stop. He rolled across the room and crashed into a mirror, smashing the mirror and the violin. But he HAD invented roller skates!

### Whiz kids
Today, roller skating is very popular. Kids whiz around their neighborhoods and they even take part in speed and dance competitions.

## Roller sport

There's a popular game played on roller skates called Roller Hockey. Each team has four players and a goalkeeper. The idea of the game is to zoom around and score as many goals as possible.

## Roller blades

Some roller skates have wheels in the center of the boot. When you balance on these wheels, it's like balancing on ice skates. Ice skaters use them to practice when they're not on the ice.

# Why are teddy bears called Teddy?

They are named after President Theodore "Teddy" Roosevelt. One day, when the President was out hunting, he refused to shoot a baby bear. This story became famous when a newspaper reported it and from then on toy bears have been called Teddy.

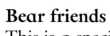

### Bear friends
This is a special teddy bear for very special children. It even has its own wheelchair.

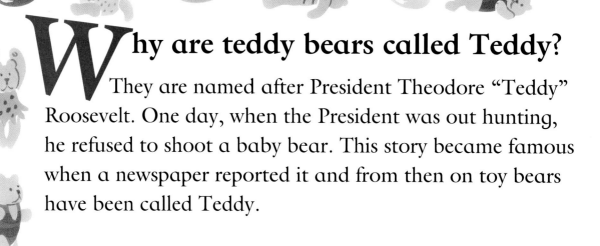

### Teddy humor
What do you get if you cross a bear with a skunk?
**Winnie-the-Pooh!**

### Pooh bear
One of the best-known toy bears is Winnie-the-Pooh. It belonged to a little boy called Christopher Milne. His Dad, A. A. Milne, wrote stories about Christopher Robin and his bear, and made them both very famous.

## Bear facts

☞ The very first toy teddy bears had humped backs, long noses and eyes made of wooden buttons. But they were still nice to cuddle!

9

# How many games can you play with cards?

Hundreds! There are at least 500 known card games, and there are probably more than that. Card games have been around a long time. All over the world people enjoy playing cards and each country has its own particular games. What's your favorite card game?

**Stop playing!**
Long ago, King Henry VIII banned card games except at Christmastime. He wanted people to get out and practice with their bows and arrows in case he decided to go to war.

## Don't breathe!

Another thing you can do with cards (very carefully) is build houses and castles.

## A game called snap

There can be two, three, or four players. The pack should be divided up equally. Without looking at their cards, each player puts one down, face upward. If two cards with the same number or type, are put down, the first person to shout "snap" wins all the cards played so far. The winner is the one who ends up with all the cards.

# What makes a top keep spinning?

After a top has been set spinning its own motion will keep it going around and around until something stops it. Air, and the tabletop or floor it is touching, will gradually slow it down to a stop. Spinning things can only stay upright as long as they are moving.

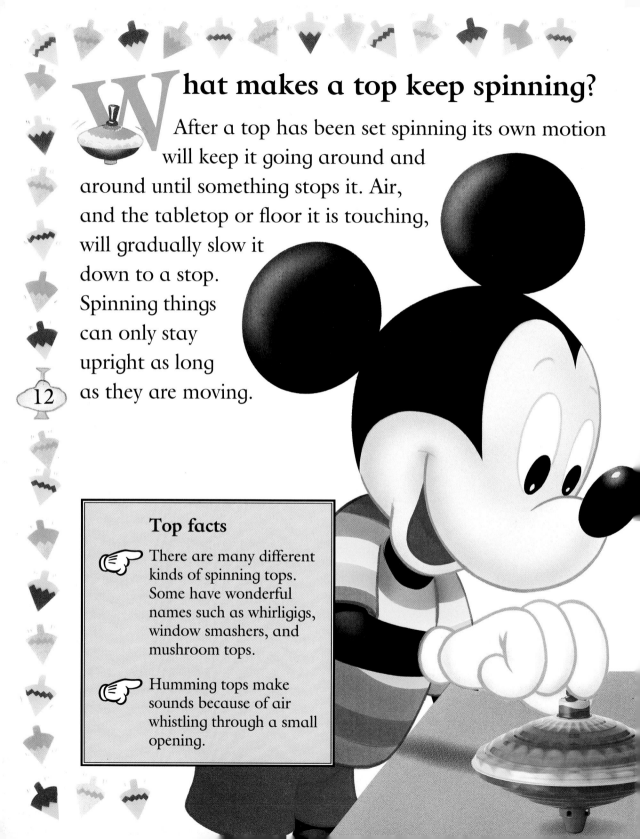

## Top facts

☞ There are many different kinds of spinning tops. Some have wonderful names such as whirligigs, window smashers, and mushroom tops.

☞ Humming tops make sounds because of air whistling through a small opening.

## Going for a spin

A gyroscope is a rotating wheel which sits on a frame. It is set spinning by a string. Its motion makes it balance evenly, like a spinning top.

# What was the world's first computer game?

It was a noisy, clunky, ENORMOUS space-war game that was invented by scientists in the 1960s. Because of its size, and the fact that it needed so much large and expensive equipment to make it work, very few people got to play it. But fortunately one man, named Nolan Bushnell, did. He thought it was so amazing that he went on to invent his own, much easier computer games that everyone could play.

14

## What's new?

When you sit down in this amazing machine, it's just like stepping INTO a computer game. The action is all around the player.

## Computer data

☞ Hand-held computer games have been popular since they were introduced in 1983.

☞ People in America spend almost five billion dollars a year on computer games.

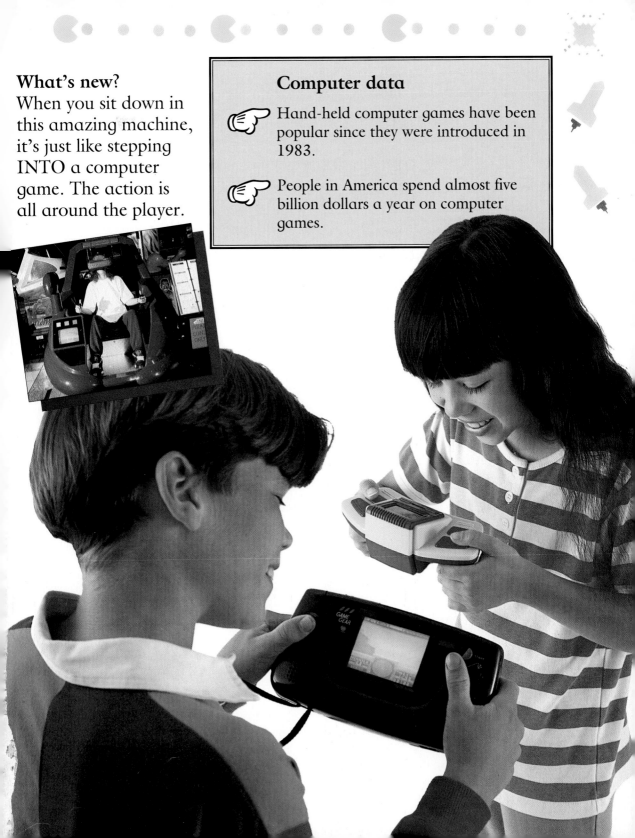

# What is the oldest game still played?

It is probably a game called Mancala which has been played in Africa and Asia for more than 3,000 years. Mancala is played by moving shells or seeds across a wooden board with 12 scoops carved in it. The object is to capture as many shells or seeds as you can.

**Playing with history**
When you play jacks, you are playing the same game that kids played in ancient Greece thousands of years ago.

**The game of Go**
Go is also a very old game from China. It's like checkers and chess all rolled into one. Japanese Samurai warriors loved to play this game. It is thought that it helped them prepare for battle.

**Buzz fun**
Here's a very old game for you to play:
The players sit in a circle and begin to count in turn, from one to one hundred. But when the number seven comes they say "buzz." If anyone forgets, they are out of the circle.

# How long have toy soldiers been around?

For over 200 years. One day, a German man named Johann Gottfried Hilpert, saw some metal workers making soldiers for their children out of leftover pieces of tin from their work. This gave him the idea to make toy soldiers for children everywhere.

**Forward march!** These toy soldiers are models of soldiers that fought in the Revolutionary War.

## Tin soldier facts

☞ There's a famous fairy story by Hans Christian Andersen called "The Tin Soldier."

☞ Grown-ups reenact famous battles using toy soldiers.

**Left, right**
Where do you find the youngest soldiers?
**In the infantry!**

## Looking at the past
These toy soldiers are models of the Union troops that fought in the Civil War.

# Have children always played with dolls?

We know that children had dolls to play with nearly 5,000 years ago in Egypt, because some clay and ivory dolls have been discovered. We also know that children in Europe had dolls long ago. The first dollmaking business started in Germany 500 years ago.

**All kinds of dolls**
There are many different kinds of dolls. There are dolls that walk, talk, sing, and play.

20

**Dolly wardrobe**
Dolls need clothes
too! Over the years
the designs of dolls'
clothes have
changed just like
people's clothes.

**Dolly facts**

☞ The Hopi Indians
of North America
carved doll figures
from cottonwood.
Then they painted the
dolls and hung them
from beams so all the
children of the tribe
could see them.

# How long is a jump rope?

As long as you like! There are long ropes for lots of kids to jump together, and there are shorter ropes for just one person. Jumping rope is a good way to have fun, and keep fit at the same time.

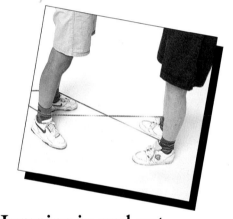

**Jumping in and out**
There are different kinds of jump ropes. This is a Chinese jump rope. It is made of elastic with the ends knotted together.

23

**Something to say while you jump!**
"My mother gave me fifty cents to see the elephant jump the fence. He jumped so high he reached the sky, and he didn't come back till the fourth of July."

### Keep on jumping

Here's another rhyme for you to say as you jump with your jump rope.
"Engine, engine number nine, going down Chicago line. If the train should jump the track, will I get my money back? Yes, no, maybe so..."

# Why do babies like rattles?

Because they LOVE that rattling noise, and rattles are easy to hold. They are also good to chew on and chewing is comforting for teething babies. Babies get a lot of pleasure from grasping things and putting them in their mouths.

**Rattle and roll**
Why is an old car like a baby?
**It never goes anywhere without a rattle.**

## Rattle history

A famous baby used to shake this rattle. His father, Napoleon Bonaparte, ruled France long ago. Fancy, isn't it?

## First toys

👉 Babies like soft toys that make a noise. They also like to look at colorful, dancing mobiles hanging above their cribs.

👉 Before toy factories started making toys, parents usually made all their children's toys by hand.

## Musical rattles

Rattles are not just used as toys. These rattles were once used as musical instruments or as part of special ceremonies.

# When were kites invented?

Kites probably first appeared in China about 3,000 years ago, but they weren't toys. Long, long ago, when the Chinese had lots of wars to fight, soldiers fitted bamboo pipes to kites. As the kites flew over the enemy, wind whistled through the pipes and scared the enemy. They ran away because they thought the strange sounds from the sky meant the gods were angry with them.

## Kite facts

In the last century, the American Weather Bureau used kites to help tell them what the weather was going to be like. They attached special instruments to the kites to test the air.

## High flying festival
Kite flying festivals are very popular. The huge, brightly colored kites make a fine display.

## Up and away
Some people have taken kite flying one step further.

# MICKEY'S Mind teaser

Look at the toys on the toy shelf. Two of the toys were once used by ancient armies. Can you remember which ones they are?

**Answers:** Kite; Yo-yo.